Two Awesome F[...]

I want to say "Thank You" for [...]
together a few, awesome free gifts for you.

[The Essential Kitchen Series Cooking Hacks & Tips Book](#)
[&](#)
[100 Delicious New Recipes](#)

These gifts are the perfect add-on to this book and I know you'll love them.

So visit the link below to grab them.

www.GoodLivingPublishing.com/essential-kitchen

Contents

Chapter 1 - Vegetarian Lunches 4
    Benefits of Vegetarian Diet 5
    Common Ingredients in Vegetarian Food 6

Chapter 2 - Salads 7
    Beet Salad 8
    Squash and Kale Salad 9
    Veggie Samosa 10
    Bean and Mango Salad 12
    Cheesy Strawberry Salad 13
    Vegetarian Barbecue Salad 14
    Sprout Salad 16
    Sweet and Spicy Salad 18
    Soba Salad 19
    Grilled Veggie Salad 20

Chapter 3 - Soups 21
    Cauliflower Curry Soup 22
    Garlicky Mushroom Soup 24
    Sweet Potato Soup 26
    Cabbage Soup 28
    Kale Squash Soup 29
    Asparagus Curry Soup 31
    Ravioli Soup 33
    Cous Cous Soup 34
    French Onion Soup 35
    Lentil Soup 37

Chapter 4 - Sandwiches 38
    Avocado Wrap 39

- Egg Salad Sandwiches 41
- Roast Tofu Sandwich 42
- Tofu Wrap 43
- Eggplant Sandwich 44
- Cheese Panini 45
- Veggie Hoagies 46
- Portobello Barbecue 47
- Torta 48
- Margherita Sandwich 49

Chapter 5 - Conclusion 50

Chapter 1 - Vegetarian Lunches

Whether you are a newcomer to the concept of vegetarianism an old hat looking for fresh new recipe ideas, you have come to the right place!

This recipe book is here to help you build your recipe repertoire or fill it out if your lunches are beginning to get boring and repetitive.

It isn't at all difficult to prepare delicious and healthy vegetarian meals. Many can even be made a few days ahead of time and stored in the refrigerator or made well ahead of time and frozen for a couple of months.

No matter what kind of recipe you are looking for, you are sure to find it within these pages!

Benefits of Vegetarian Diet

Vegetarian dieting has tons of great benefits. As soon as you cut meat out of your diet, you will definitely notice a difference in your life!

If you are concerned with animal welfare, of course, eating a meatless diet will make you feel much better about your relationship with animals in no time. However, even if that is not a priority for you, you can still feel much better about yourself knowing that you are putting healthy and fresh foods into your body every single day. And if you have a farmer's market nearby, you can buy your produce there and support local businesses, too!

Cutting out meat from your diet will also make your mind much clearer and help you focus on your work. When you eat a healthy, nutrient-rich diet, your brain benefits as much as your body does. If you need more energy and better concentration every day, try eating vegetarian food. You won't regret it!

Lastly, a vegetarian diet will help your body feel great as well. You will lose weight easily when you remove fatty meats from your diet, and your body will benefit from the increased intake of antioxidants, vitamins, and nutrients that you receive from eating foods rich with fruits and vegetables. Any way you look at it, a vegetarian diet is great for you!

Common Ingredients in Vegetarian Food

For easy food preparation any time, keep your refrigerator and pantry well stocked with these items!

- Olive oil
- Quinoa (dry)
- Salt and pepper
- Dried seasonings of your choosing
- Fresh seasonings of your choosing
- Lemon juice
- Frozen veggies
- Canned beans
- Honey
- Rice (dry)
- Vegetable broth
- Breads
- Brown sugar
- Mayonnaise

Chapter 2 - Salads

No vegetarian diet would be complete without fresh and delicious salads for lunch every now and then!

Store these salads in mason jars and combine with your favorite dressing when you're ready to eat them!

Beet Salad

Serve up a hearty beet salad that is full of fall flavor!

Serves: 2

Ingredients

- 2 tbsp olive oil
- Pinch of sea salt
- 1 pound beets
- 2 cups cooked quinoa
- 1 minced clove of garlic
- 1/4 cup diced red onion
- 4 chopped fresh basil leaves
- 1/2 cup feta cheese
- 1/4 cup pumpkin seeds

Instructions

Preheat oven to 400 degrees Fahrenheit.

Peel and cube beets; place in a baking dish and drizzle with olive oil and sea salt.

Bake for 20 minutes, then let cool.

Toss cooked quinoa with basil, feta, red onion, pumpkin seeds, and garlic, then fold in beets.

Serve.

Squash and Kale Salad

Kale is the health food craze that everyone is talking about. Get plenty in your diet with this recipe!

Serves: 4

Ingredients

- 3 tbsp olive oil
- 1 peeled, seeded, and diced butternut squash
- 1 bunch torn kale
- 1 tsp salt
- 1 tsp black pepper
- 1/3 cup water
- 1/3 cup tahini
- 1 cup cooked lentils
- 2 tbsp lemon juice
- 1 cup pita chips

Instructions

Preheat oven to 425 degrees Fahrenheit.

Toss squash with 1 tbsp olive oil, pepper, and salt, then place on baking sheet and roast for 30 minutes, stirring once.

Drizzle 1 tbsp olive oil over kale, then massage for 5 minutes.

Whisk remaining olive oil together with tahini, lemon juice, and water.

Toss all ingredients together.

Serve.

Veggie Samosa

Enjoy this cooked chickpea salad warm or cool—it's great either way!

Serves: 2

Ingredients

    4 cups lettuce
    1 bunch sliced carrots
    2 sliced shallots
    1 pound diced potatoes
    1 cup fresh peas
    1 tsp curry
    1 cup chickpeas
    1 tsp cumin
    1 tsp red pepper flakes
    1 tsp garlic powder
    2 tbsp olive oil
    1/2 cup ginger dressing

Instructions

Preheat oven to 400 degrees Fahrenheit.

Rinse and dry chickpeas, then toss with olive oil, curry, cumin, garlic powder, and red pepper flakes.

Place on a baking sheet on the bottom rack of the oven and roast for 20 minutes.

Toss carrots and potatoes with olive oil, then spread on a second baking sheet and roast on middle oven rack for 20 minutes.

Toss lettuce, peas, shallots, toasted chickpeas, and roasted carrots and potatoes in a large bowl.

Serve topped with ginger dressing.

Bean and Mango Salad

This tasty salad can be thrown together in less than 10 minutes!

Serves: 4

Ingredients

1 mango
15oz canned rinsed and drained black beans
1 zucchini
1 jalapeño pepper
1/4 cup cilantro
2 tbsp lime juice
1 tbsp olive oil
1 tsp salt
1 tsp black pepper

Instructions

Peel and chop mango into bite-sized pieces.

Thinly slice zucchini.

Mince jalapeño.

Chop cilantro.

Combine all ingredients into a large bowl and toss to combine thoroughly.

Serve.

Cheesy Strawberry Salad

Fresh summertime flavors collide in this feta and strawberry dish!

Serves: 2

Ingredients

- 3 cups mixed greens
- 3 cups spinach
- 1/3 cup sliced almonds
- 1 cup sliced strawberries
- 1/3 cup crumbled feta cheese
- 1/2 sliced red onion
- 1/4 cup balsamic vinaigrette dressing

Instructions

Combine mixed greens and spinach with almonds, strawberries, and onion in a large bowl.

Toss in vinaigrette dressing to combine thoroughly.

Serve topped with sliced strawberries and crumbled feta cheese.

Optionally, toss cheese and strawberries into salad to combine everything.

Vegetarian Barbecue Salad

Even picky eaters are sure to love this barbecued tofu lunch!

Serves: 2

Ingredients

1 package tofu
1 chopped head of romaine lettuce
1 grilled corn on the cob
1 grilled onion
2 grilled red bell peppers
2 grilled zucchinis
2 grilled jalapeño peppers
3 chopped cucumbers
15 halved cherry tomatoes
1/2 sliced jicama
2 chopped scallions
1 diced avocado
3/4 cup barbecue sauce

Instructions

Brush corn on the cob, onion, red bell peppers, zucchinis, and jalapeño peppers with olive oil, then grill over medium-high until charred; chop vegetables and remove corn kernels from cob.

Toss grilled vegetables with lettuce, cucumbers, jicama, scallions, avocado, and tomato in a large bowl.

Dice tofu and place in a skillet over medium heat.

Stir tofu with barbecue sauce and cook for 10 minutes.

Toss tofu with vegetables in large bowl and top with extra barbecue sauce.

Serve.

Sprout Salad

You'll actually look forward to eating your Brussels sprouts when you chow down on this lunch!

Serves: 2

Ingredients

    1-1/2 cups cubed stale bread
    1 pound Brussels sprouts
    1/4 cup olive oil
    1 tsp honey
    1/4 tsp chili flakes
    3 tbsp lemon juice
    2 eggs
    1/2 cup grated Parmesan cheese
    1 tbsp white vinegar

Instructions

Preheat oven to 350 degrees Fahrenheit.

Shred Brussels sprouts and place in a bowl.

Spread bread cubes onto a baking sheet and coat with olive oil.

Bake for 10 minutes or until lightly golden.

Cook chili flakes for 5 minutes in 1/4 cup olive oil in a skillet over medium heat, then strain.

Whisk lemon juice and honey into strained oil.

Simmer 3 inches of water over medium-low heat, then stir in vinegar.

Crack eggs into a small bowl, then stir with the end of a spoon.

Drop eggs into water and cook for 4 minutes to poach.

Toss Brussels sprouts with croutons, cheese, and dressing.

Serve topped with poached egg.

Sweet and Spicy Salad

Peaches and peppers learn to get along in this tasty recipe.

Serves: 4

Ingredients

    1 cup rinsed quinoa
    2 cups water
    1 minced shallot
    1 jalapeño pepper
    1 juiced lime
    2 tbsp olive oil
    2 tbsp white wine vinegar
    4 peaches
    2oz goat cheese
    8 cups salad greens

Instructions

Boil quinoa in water, then reduce heat and simmer for 10 minutes.

Cook jalapeño in a cast iron skillet over high heat for 8 minutes to blacken, then let cool.

Mince pepper, discarding seeds.

In a small jar, combine shallot, pepper, vinegar, lime juice, and oil; cover and shake to combine.

Cut peaches in half, remove the pits, and place on a grill or grill pan on high heat for 5 minutes; slice grilled peaches.

Toss greens with quinoa and dressing.

Serve topped with grilled peaches and goat cheese.

Soba Salad

Get some Asian flavor in your life with this healthy and light lunch recipe!

Serves: 2

Ingredients

- 1 bunch broccolini
- 1/2 package soba noodles
- 1 chopped yellow bell pepper
- 1/4 cup sliced basil leaves
- 2/3 cup sliced sun-dried tomatoes
- 1/4 cup balsamic vinaigrette dressing

Instructions

Cook noodles according to packaging directions.

Place broccolini in a pot on the stove with two inches of cold water; cover and bring to a boil to steam for 4 minutes.

Drain broccolini and place in ice water, then chop and toss with sun-dried tomatoes and pepper.

Drain noodles and let cool somewhat.

Toss noodles with dressing, then toss with vegetable mixture.

Stir in basil leaves.

Serve.

Grilled Veggie Salad

If you have a little extra time to prepare your lunch, go for this fresh grilled veggie salad. You'll be glad you did!

Serves: 4

Ingredients

- 3 zucchinis
- 1 bunch trimmed asparagus
- 12oz baby greens
- 2 bell peppers
- 1/2 cup olive oil
- 3/4 cup shredded Parmesan cheese
- 1 tsp salt
- 1 tsp black pepper
- 1/4 cup canola oil
- 3 tbsp balsamic vinegar
- 2 tbsp honey

Instructions

Toss vegetables with pepper, salt, and olive oil in a large bowl.

Grill until charred on a grill or grill pan.

Whisk together 1/4 cup olive oil, canola oil, honey, and balsamic vinegar until combined thoroughly.

Remove vegetables and chop into small pieces.

Toss veggies with dressing, cheese, and greens.

Serve.

Chapter 3 - Soups

Have a healthy and hearty bowl of vegetarian soup for lunch, or pair it with a salad for a bigger meal!

These can be made ahead of time and kept in mason jars in the refrigerator, or frozen in sealable plastic baggies until ready to reheat and eat.

Cauliflower Curry Soup

This creamy soup is infused with tons of Thai flavor!

Serves: 4

Ingredients

    1 cup chopped and washed leeks
    2 tbsp olive oil
    1-1/2 pounds cauliflower florets
    1/3 cup chopped cilantro
    2 tsp salt
    1 tbsp basmati rice
    2 tbsp green curry paste
    1 inch piece of fresh grated ginger
    1 tbsp lemongrass paste
    1 can coconut milk
    Water to make 4 cups coconut milk
    2 tbsp lime juice
    2 tbsp coconut butter

Instructions

Cook cilantro, leeks, rice, cauliflower, and 1-1/2 tsp salt in oil in a pot on the stove over medium-low heat for 5 minutes.

In a large bowl, stir together ginger, curry paste, and lemongrass paste, then beat in water and coconut milk.

Pour mixture into the pot of vegetables and bring to a boil over high heat.

Reduce heat to medium-low, cover partially, and simmer for 25 minutes.

Place 2 cups of the soup into a blender; blend on high until smooth, then stir back into the soup.

Stir in lime juice and remaining salt, then stir in coconut butter and remove from heat.

Serve.

Garlicky Mushroom Soup

This is a perfect fall and winter soup, as it is packed full of hearty flavor to warm you from the inside out.

Serves: 4

Ingredients

1 tbsp butter
1 tbsp olive oil
1 chopped onion
2 chopped heads of garlic
1 peeled and chopped apple
1 handful parsley
1 quart vegetable broth
1/2 tsp salt
1/2 tsp dill weed
1/2 tsp mustard powder
1 pound sliced button mushrooms
1/2 cup cream
1/4 tsp black pepper

Instructions

Cook onions and garlic in a pot on the stove over medium-low heat in oil for 25 minutes.

Add apple, stir, and cook 10 more minutes.

Add herbs and stock and bring to a boil; reduce heat to low and simmer 15 minutes.

Remove herbs and place soup in a blender; blend on high until smooth.

Add dill, mustard powder, black pepper, and salt, then heat soup through on low heat.

Cook mushrooms in a separate skillet until slightly brown, then pour into soup.

Stir in cream, then remove soup from heat.

Serve.

Sweet Potato Soup

This unique soup is as gluten-free as it is vegetarian!

Serves: 4

Ingredients

- 1 tbsp red curry paste
- 1 tbsp olive oil
- 1/2 tsp cinnamon
- 4 cloves minced garlic
- 1 peeled and diced red onion
- 1 peeled and diced sweet potato
- 1 seeded and diced jalapeño pepper
- 1 seeded and diced yellow bell pepper
- 1 quart vegetable broth
- 1/2 pound cooked black beans
- 1/2 cup boiling water
- 1/2 cup peanut butter
- 1/2 tsp red pepper flakes
- 1 lime
- 2 tbsp chopped fresh cilantro
- 3 tsp brown sugar

Instructions

Cook curry paste and cinnamon in olive oil in a large pot on the stove over medium heat for 1 minute, stirring.

Add garlic, onion, bell pepper, sweet potato, and jalapeño pepper; stir and cook for 7 minutes to soften.

Add broth and beans; stir.

Mix peanut butter with boiling water, then stir mixture into soup along with cilantro and red pepper flakes.

Bring to a boil; cover and simmer for 25 minutes.

Stir in brown sugar and lime juice.

Serve.

Cabbage Soup

This brilliantly green soup is so full of flavor you'll never want to stop eating it!

Serves: 2

Ingredients

    1 chopped potato
    1 chopped onion
    2 tbsp Greek yogurt
    3 tbsp olive oil
    2 cups vegetable broth
    5 savoy cabbages, cut into strips
    2 slices bread
    2 tbsp grated Leicester cheese

Instructions

Cook onion and potatoes in olive oil in a pot over medium heat for 5 minutes.

Turn heat to low; cover and cook 10 minutes, then add stock.

Bring to a boil and add cabbage, then simmer for 10 more minutes.

Add soup to blender; blend on high until smooth.

Serve topped with cheese.

Kale Squash Soup

Join the kale revolution with this yummy recipe!

Serves: 4

Ingredients

    1 butternut squash
    1 bunch curly kale, chopped
    3 carrots, peeled and sliced
    1-1/2 cups cooked and drained chickpeas
    1 chopped piece of fresh ginger root
    1 chopped yellow onion
    1 sprig fresh rosemary
    4 cups vegetable broth
    5 chopped sage leaves
    2 tbsp coconut oil
    1 cup water
    1 tsp salt
    1 tsp black pepper

Instructions

Preheat oven to 425 degrees Fahrenheit.

Halve squash and place on a baking sheet; roast for 20 minutes.

Cook onion in oil for 5 minutes in a large pot on the stove over medium heat.

Stir in carrots and ginger and cook for 5 more minutes.

Stir in water, broth, chickpeas, salt, and herbs and bring to a boil, then reduce heat to low and cook, covered, for 20 minutes.

Remove squash from oven and let cool, then peel and cut into small pieces.

Stir squash into soup with kale; cover and cook 10 more minutes.

Serve.

Asparagus Curry Soup

Make up a bowl of this green soup in the early spring when fresh asparagus is abundant!

Serves: 4

Ingredients

    2/3 cup raw cashews
    1 diced onion
    1 tbsp olive oil
    2 minced cloves of garlic
    2 pounds trimmed and diced asparagus
    1 tbsp sweet curry powder
    6 cups vegetable broth
    Lemon juice as wanted
    Salt and pepper as wanted

Instructions

Soak cashews in hot water while preparing the soup.

Cook onion in olive oil in a skillet over medium-high heat for 5 minutes.

Stir in garlic and curry powder and cook for 1 more minute.

Add asparagus and broth; bring to a boil and reduce heat to low.

Simmer for 15 minutes.

Rinse cashews and place in blender; add a bit of the soup and blend until smooth.

Place remaining soup in blender and blend until creamy.

Return all soup to the pot and heat through on medium.

Season with salt, pepper, and lemon juice as desired.

Serve.

Ravioli Soup

Use cheese-only ravioli to make this soup veggie-friendly!

Serves: 4

Ingredients

- 2 cups frozen pepper and onion mix, thawed
- 1 tbsp olive oil
- 2 cloves minced garlic
- 28oz canned crushed fire roasted tomatoes
- 1/4 tsp crushed red pepper
- 15oz canned vegetable broth
- 1-1/2 cups hot water
- 9oz frozen or fresh cheese ravioli
- 1 tsp dried basil
- 1 tsp black pepper
- 2 cups diced zucchini

Instructions

Heat oil over medium heat in a large pot; cook garlic, pepper and onion mix, and red pepper and cook for 1 minute.

Add water, basil, broth, and tomatoes and bring to a rolling boil over high heat.

Add ravioli and cook for 3 minutes less than what it recommends on the package.

Add zucchini and return to a boil; cook 3 minutes.

Season with black pepper and serve.

Cous Cous Soup

This soup cooks up in the slow cooker, making it a great dish to prepare when you're extra busy!

Serves: 2

Ingredients

   30oz canned drained red kidney beans
   1 cup uncooked pearl couscous
   1 cup chopped carrots
   1 tbsp butter
   1 chopped onion
   1 chopped green bell pepper
   1 cup spaghetti sauce
   15oz canned diced tomatoes
   1 tsp dried oregano
   1/4 tsp black pepper
   1 tsp salt
   32oz vegetable broth

Instructions

Cook pepper, onions, and carrots in skillet in melted butter over medium-high heat for 15 minutes.

Place vegetables in slow cooker.

Stir all remaining ingredients into the slow cooker so that the flavors will combine thoroughly.

Cover and cook on low for 2 hours.

Serve.

French Onion Soup

Not only is this recipe completely vegetarian, it's also only got about a third of the amount of fat found in regular French Onion Soup!

Serves: 6

Ingredients

- 1 tbsp vegetable oil
- 2 tbsp butter
- 3 minced cloves garlic
- 5 chopped onions
- 1/2 tsp salt
- 6 cups vegetable broth
- 2 tbsp flour
- 1 tsp Dijon mustard
- 1/3 cup dry sherry
- 1 tsp sherry vinegar
- 2/3 cup shredded Gruyere cheese
- 6 slices toasted sourdough bread

Instructions

Melt butter and oil together in a skillet over medium heat; cook garlic, onions, and salt for 5 minutes.

Turn to low and cook for 1 hour, stirring occasionally.

Stir in flour and continue stirring while cooking for 4 minutes.

Stir in mustard, sherry, and broth; cover and simmer 15 minutes, then stir in sherry vinegar.

Preheat oven broiler.

Spoon soup into bowls and top with toast and cheese.

Broil for 2 minutes.

Serve.

Lentil Soup

Hearty lentils provide the base for this warm and wonderful soup recipe.

Serves: 6

Ingredients

- 4 leeks, sliced
- 1 bunch kale, stems removed, chopped into ribbons
- 28oz canned whole tomatoes, drained
- 1 tbsp olive oil
- 1/2 cup brown lentils
- 2 diced and peeled sweet potatoes
- 2 tsp salt
- 1/4 tsp black pepper
- 1 tbsp thyme
- 12 basil leaves
- 1/4 cup grated Parmesan cheese

Instructions

Cook leeks in oil in a skillet over medium heat for 3 minutes.

Add tomatoes and cook for 5 minutes, breaking up as you go.

Add water and bring to a boil, then stir in sweet potatoes, kale, thyme, lentils, pepper, salt, and basil.

Simmer for 30 minutes.

Serve topped with Parmesan.

Chapter 4 - Sandwiches

Want something a little different than soup or salad for lunch today?

Reach for one of these recipes and you're sure to be satisfied!

Avocado Wrap

Grab a tasty, crunchy wrap filled with energizing avocado for your midday meal!

Serves: 4

Ingredients

    1 tbsp canola oil
    2 tbsp cider vinegar
    1/4 tsp salt
    2 tsp chopped chipotle chile pepper in adobo sauce
    2 cups shredded red cabbage
    1/4 cup chopped fresh cilantro
    1 shredded carrot
    1 peeled and pitted avocado
    15oz canned drained and rinsed white beans
    2 tbsp minced red onion
    1/2 cup shredded sharp cheddar cheese
    4 wheat tortillas

Instructions

In a large bowl, whisk together oil, vinegar, salt, and chipotle pepper.

Stir in cilantro, cabbage, and carrot and toss to combine thoroughly.

Mash avocado together with beans in a separate bowl, then stir in onion and cheese.

On each wrap, spread 1/2 cup bean mixture and top with 2/3 cup cabbage slaw.

Roll each wrap tightly, tucking in ends.

Slice in half and serve.

Egg Salad Sandwiches

Serve up some smooth egg salad for a tasty lunchtime treat!

Serves: 2

Ingredients

    4 slices toasted bread
    6 eggs
    1/4 cup mayonnaise
    4 tbsp Dijon mustard
    2 tsp dill weed
    1 tsp black pepper

Instructions

Boil eggs in water on the stove over high heat; remove from heat and let stand, covered, for 15 minutes, then rinse with cold water.

Mash eggs in a bowl with mayonnaise, mustard, pepper, and dill weed.

Spread onto toasted bread.

Serve.

Roast Tofu Sandwich

These unique sandwiches have a unique Asian flavor that can't be beat!

Serves: 2

Ingredients

14oz package drained extra-firm tofu
1/3 cup lime juice
1/3 cup soy sauce
3 tbsp toasted sesame oil
4 slices toasted bread

Instructions

Cut tofu into small cubes.

Toss tofu with lime juice, soy sauce, and oil in a bowl.

Marinate for 1 to 4 hours.

Preheat oven to 450 degrees Fahrenheit.

Remove tofu from marinade and spread onto a baking sheet.

Roast for 20 minutes, turning halfway through.

Top 2 slices of toast with tofu.

Close sandwiches and serve.

Tofu Wrap

A tasty on-the-go Thai dish is just moments away!

Serves: 1

Ingredients

    1 wheat tortilla
    1/4 cup sliced red bell pepper
    8 sliced snow peas
    2oz sliced baked tofu
    1 tbsp Thai peanut sauce

Instructions

Spread peanut sauce onto tortilla.

In the center, arrange tofu, snow peas, and peppers.

Tuck in sides of tortilla, then roll up starting with the edge facing away from you.

Slice and serve.

Eggplant Sandwich

This recipe will help you create a restaurant-worthy eggplant sandwich any time, every time!

Serves: 4

Ingredients

    1/4 cup mayonnaise
    1 chopped clove of garlic
    1 sliced eggplant
    1 tsp lemon juice
    3 Portobello mushroom caps, gills removed
    1/2 tsp salt
    1/2 tsp black pepper
    2 cups arugula
    1 sliced tomato
    8 slices wheat bread

Instructions

Preheat grill or grill pan to medium-high.

Stir garlic into mayonnaise and lemon juice.

Season eggplant and mushroom with salt and pepper.

Grill vegetables for 3 minutes per side.

Spread garlic mayonnaise onto bread.

Layer mushrooms, eggplant, arugula, and tomato on sandwiches.

Close sandwiches and serve.

Cheese Panini

Add a spicy kick to your cheese Panini for a tasty southwest meal!

Serves: 4

Ingredients

1 cup shredded zucchini
4oz shredded sharp cheddar cheese
1/4 cup chopped red onion
1/2 cup shredded carrot
1/4 cup salsa
8 slices wheat bread
1 tbsp chopped pickled jalapeño pepper
2 tsp canola oil

Instructions

In a large bowl, stir together zucchini, cheddar, onion, carrot, jalapeño, and salsa.

Divide between 4 slices of bread, then close sandwiches with remaining pieces of bread.

Place Panini sandwiches in olive oil in a skillet over medium heat, then top with another skillet weighed down with cans.

Cook Panini for 2 minutes per side.

Alternately, press in a Panini press.

Serve.

Veggie Hoagies

No need to stuff your hoagies with meat! Enjoy these vegetable hoagies with very little prep time!

Serves: 4

Ingredients

- 14oz chopped and rinsed can of artichoke hearts
- 1/4 cup sliced red onion rings
- 2 tbsp balsamic vinegar
- 1 seeded and diced tomato
- 1 tsp dried oregano
- 1 tbsp olive oil
- 2 slices provolone cheese, halved
- 16inch baguette
- 2 cups shredded romaine lettuce

Instructions

Stir together tomato, artichoke hearts, oregano, vinegar, and oil in a large bowl.

Cut baguette into 4 lengths, then split and remove bread from inside.

Lay half a slice of provolone on each sandwich, then top with artichoke mixture and sliced onion. Finish with lettuce.

Close sandwiches and serve.

Portobello Barbecue

Make a tasty, saucy Portobello barbecue quesadilla for a lunch everyone will envy!

Serves: 4

Ingredients

    1 tbsp tomato paste
    1/2 cup barbecue sauce
    1 tbsp cider vinegar
    1 tbsp and 2 tsp canola oil
    1 chipotle chile in adobo sauce, minced
    1 diced onion
    1 pound Portobello mushroom cups, diced and gills removed
    3/4 cup shredded Monterey Jack cheese
    4 wheat tortillas

Instructions

Stir together tomato paste, barbecue sauce, chipotle, and vinegar in a large bowl.

Cook mushrooms in 1 tbsp oil in a skillet over medium heat for 5 minutes.

Add onion, then cook for 5 minutes more.

Stir vegetables into barbecue sauce mixture.

Spread 3 tbsp cheese on each tortilla and top with 1/2 cup filling.

Fold in half and press to flatten.

Cook quesadillas in 1 tsp oil for 2 minutes per side each.

Torta

Tortas are usually stuffed with meat; make a change with this bean-based recipe!

Serves: 4

Ingredients

3 tbsp salsa
15oz canned drained and rinsed black beans
1 tbsp chopped pickled jalapeño pepper
1 pitted avocado
1/2 tsp ground cumin
1 tbsp lime juice
2 tbsp minced onion
1-1/3 cup shredded green cabbage
16inch baguette

Instructions

Mash together beans, cumin, jalapeño, and salsa in a large bowl

Mash together onion, avocado, and lime juice in a separate small bowl.

Slice baguette into four lengths, then slice in half horizontally and pull out most of the center.

Divide the two mashed mixtures between the sandwiches.

Cut in half and serve.

Margherita Sandwich

This incredibly easy sandwich will give you tons of Tuscan flavor in no time!

Serves: 2

Ingredients

    1/2 cup sun-dried tomatoes
    2 tbsp Dijon mustard
    1 tbsp oil from sun-dried tomatoes
    1/2 loaf split and hollowed ciabatta bread
    8 leaves romaine lettuce
    1/2 cup parsley leaves
    6oz sliced fresh mozzarella
    1 tsp salt
    1 tsp black pepper

Instructions

Whisk together mustard and oil until thick, then spread over bread.

Layer bread bottoms with lettuce, cheese, tomatoes, and parsley, then sprinkle black pepper and salt over.

Close sandwich.

Wrap in plastic wrap and place on a baking sheet; top with another baking sheet, weighed down with a heavy skillet or canned goods.

Alternately: press in a Panini press.

Refrigerate sandwich for 1 hour, then slice and serve.

Chapter 5 - Conclusion

Are you ready for lunch then?

Just pick your favorite recipe from this book, grab your ingredients, and start cooking!

You'll be eating a vegetarian diet and effortlessly incorporating these recipes into your daily routine in no time.

Have fun, and enjoy the journey to a happier, healthier you!

Two Awesome Free Gifts For You

I want to say "Thank You" for buying my book so I've put together a few, awesome free gifts for you.

The Essential Kitchen Series Cooking Hacks & Tips Book
&
100 Delicious New Recipes

These gifts are the perfect add-on to this book and I know you'll love them.

So visit the link below to grab them.

www.GoodLivingPublishing.com/essential-kitchen

All rights Reserved. No part of this publication or the information in it may be quoted from or reproduced in any form by means such as printing, scanning, photocopying or otherwise without prior written permission of the copyright holder.

Disclaimer and Terms of Use: Effort has been made to ensure that the information in this book is accurate and complete, however, the author and the publisher do not warrant the accuracy of the information, text and graphics contained within the book due to the rapidly changing nature of science, research, known and unknown facts and internet. The Author and the publisher do not hold any responsibility for errors, omissions or contrary interpretation of the subject matter herein. This book is presented solely for motivational and informational purposes only.

Printed in Great Britain
by Amazon